WIND-UPS

Chris Ollerenshaw and Pat Triggs
Photographs by Peter J. Millard

Contents

Words that appear in the glossary are printed in
boldface type the first time they occur in the text.

Gareth Stevens Publishing
MILWAUKEE

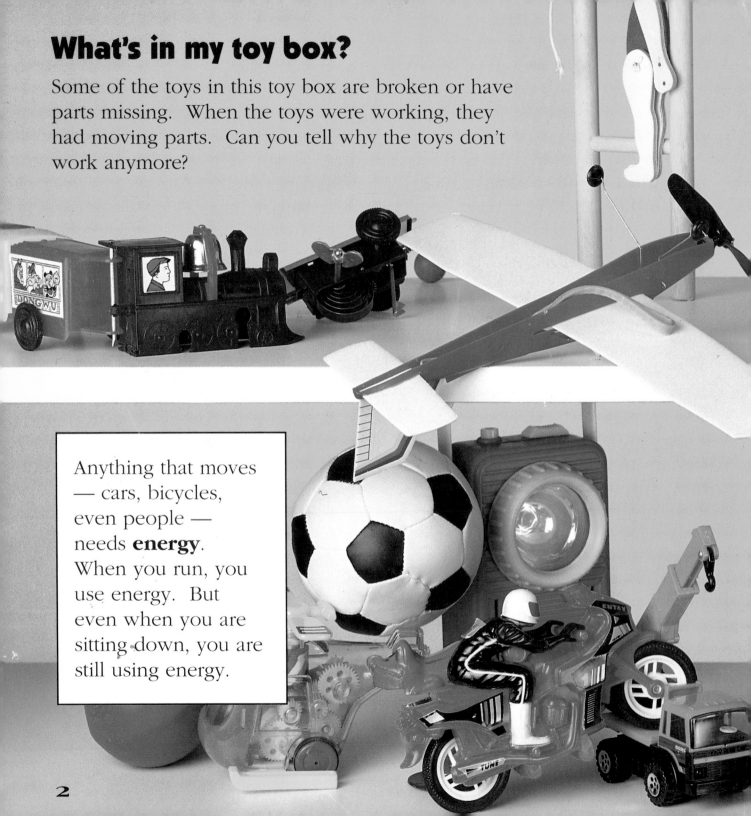

What's in my toy box?

Some of the toys in this toy box are broken or have parts missing. When the toys were working, they had moving parts. Can you tell why the toys don't work anymore?

Anything that moves — cars, bicycles, even people — needs **energy**. When you run, you use energy. But even when you are sitting down, you are still using energy.

Where do you get the energy that moves your body? You make energy from the food you eat. You store the energy in your body. When you talk, walk, or breathe, you use stored energy. Your body turns it into **kinetic** energy, or movement.

Where do these toys get the energy that makes them move?

3

Stretch, bounce, and bend

People have discovered how to use different kinds of energy to make things move.

Can you figure out how these machines work? There is something they both have in common.

These machines work because parts of them can be stretched, which stores energy, and then let go, which releases energy.

4

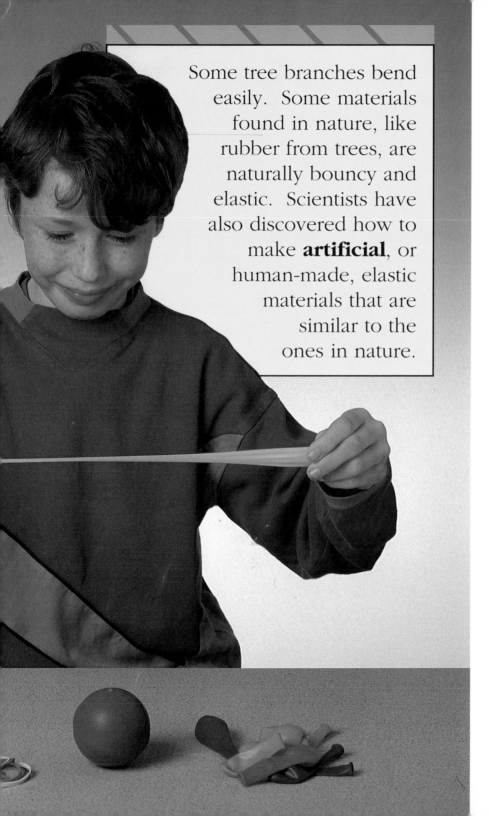

Some tree branches bend easily. Some materials found in nature, like rubber from trees, are naturally bouncy and elastic. Scientists have also discovered how to make **artificial**, or human-made, elastic materials that are similar to the ones in nature.

Can you think of any natural or artificial materials that can stretch, bounce, or bend?

A powerful energy source

To operate a slingshot, put an object into a
pouch on a sling. Then pull the sling back.
This action stores energy. The energy is held
in the tightly stretched sling.

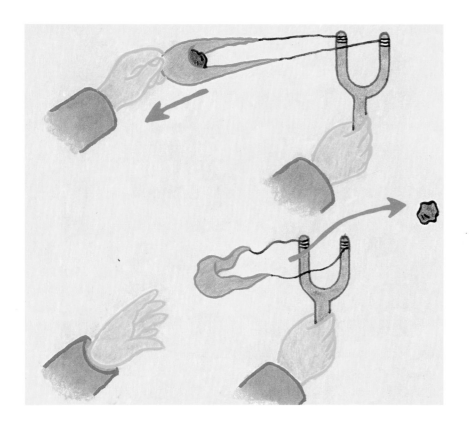

When the sling is released, the stored energy
is changed into kinetic energy. The sling
snaps back, pushing hard on the object,
which goes flying. Such powerful energy
makes the slingshot dangerous. *Never* point
it toward anything, particularly living things.

You can make a simple slingshot by stretching a rubber band between your finger and thumb. *Be careful.* Even a rubber band can hurt you or another living thing. Even the smallest and lightest missile can be harmful.

Do you see how this machine works?

Bouncing and squeezing

The energy in this jack-in-the-box is held in a squeezed cube of foam rubber.

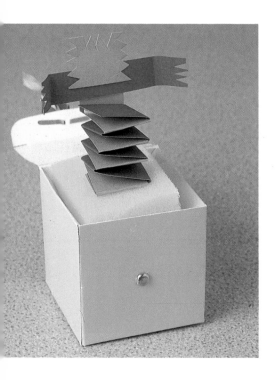

Gather some balls made of different materials. Squeeze each ball in your hand. Are some harder than others? Do some spring back quicker than others? Drop them from the same height onto different surfaces, such as concrete, carpeting, a tabletop, and a cushion. Why do you think some bounce higher?

You can make your own jack-in-the-box. How might you use the stretchiness in a rubber band to allow the lid of the box to lift so that your jack-in-the-box figure can spring up?

Holding and releasing energy

You can control the way this toy moves by the amount of energy you use. The harder you squeeze the handle, the tighter this action makes the string at the top. As you relax, the string loosens and twists.

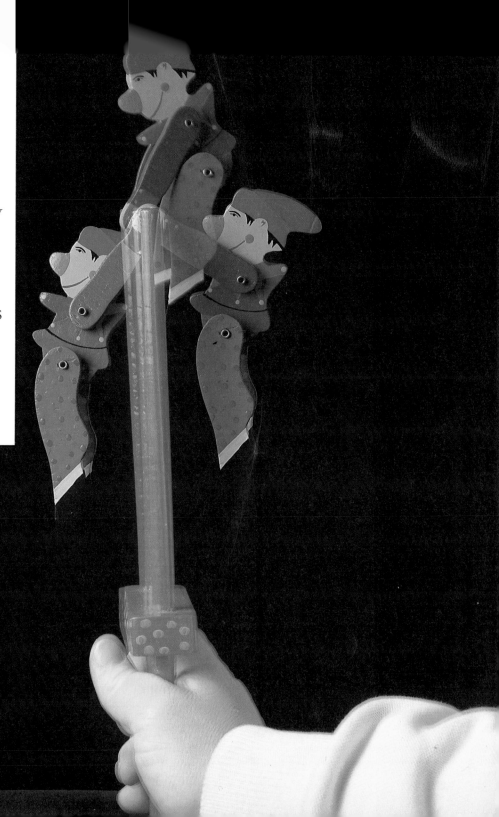

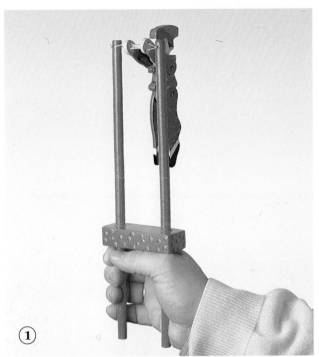

(1)

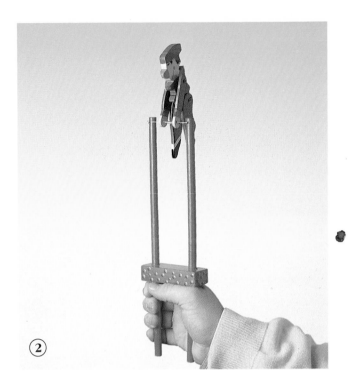

(2)

(3)

What is happening to the handle, the string, and the acrobat in each of the steps pictured on this page?

Energy in springs

Various types of metals differ as to how much stretch and bounce they have. If a piece of metal wire is not very bouncy, it can be made more so by coiling it around until a spring is made.

Take a look at different springs – from a pen, a stapler, an old clock, a lamp, and more. Find some that are not made of twisted metal and some that are not even made of metal. How many different kinds can you find?

Make a collection of toys that operate with a spring. The spring in some of the toys may be easier to locate than in others.

This toy works because of a metal spring hidden in the base of the toy. When you push the base with your finger, the toy animal, which is pieced together with string, collapses.

13

Springs for comfort

Springiness can make life much more comfortable. If you would have traveled along a bumpy road in this old cart, you would have felt each jolt. The wheels have wood and metal rims.

This carriage was designed so that the cab hung from straps. The straps acted like springs to cushion the passengers from bumps.

If you look under modern cars and trucks, you can see that they have springs built into them for comfort. The wheels on modern cars are covered with tires filled with springy air. There are springs in the seats, too. Traveling in these vehicles is much more comfortable than traveling in vehicles of the past.

Look under the seat of a bicycle to see the springs. Some bicycles also have wider tires than others. Wide rubber tires absorb more bumps than narrow tires do. See if you can discover more ways in which springiness and stretchiness make life comfortable. Look at your bed. Does it have springs, or is it made of foam rubber or some other springy material?

Making things move

You can combine stretching with twisting or winding up to make another energy-storing device.

To make this toy: cut a hole in the bottom of a plastic bottle and thread a rubber band through. Slip a *short* pencil through the loop of the rubber band that is poking through the bottom of the bottle to stop it from slipping out.

Pull the rubber band through the neck of the bottle. To make this easier, you could cut the bottle in half first, as pictured.

16

Place a large bead on the top of the bottle. Now thread the rubber band through the hole in the bead. If your bottle was cut in half, fit the top half into the bottom half.

Slip another pencil through the loop of the band that is poking through the bead. This pencil is now attached to the bead like a propeller. Turn the propeller around and around so that it twists the rubber band. Then place the bottle on its side on a tabletop and let the propeller go. Watch how your machine moves. What do you think is making it move like that?

This toy airplane works in a similar way. Energy is held in the twisted rubber band. When the band is released, the spinning propeller pushes back on the surrounding air as it pulls the plane forward.

Keeping movement going

To make a spinner, you will need a cardboard circle with two holes in its center and some string.

Thread the string through the two holes to make a loop. Then tie the ends of the string together. Hold a loop in each hand and wind up the string by flicking the spinner over and over.

When the string is nicely twisted, pull your hands apart and tighten the string. As the string unwinds, the spinner will whizz around. You can keep it going by pulling on the string before it is completely unwound and then relaxing again.

What is making the spinner work? It is getting all of its energy from the work you are doing with your muscles. The twisted string holds some of this energy for a short time. Did you notice that you had to work harder to *get* your spinner going than to *keep* it going? Why does this happen?

Did you notice that your spinner made noise? That is because the stored energy in the wound-up string changed into movement and sound energy when you released it.

Explore making more spinners. Try using different sizes, shapes, and materials. What differences do you notice each time you change the design?

Winding things up

Wind-up toys work by turning a knob or a key.

The toys then operate on the energy that is stored in a spring.

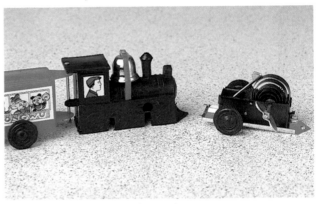

What do you think happens inside a toy like this one when you turn the key?

If you could take the toy apart, you could see what happens.

The key turns in a coil of metal. This is another kind of spring. Look at the spring when it's wound up and ready to go.

Look at it when it has run down. What changes do you see?

Turning the key of a wind-up toy tightens a spring. As the spring unwinds, the toy uses this stored energy and moves.

Collect some wind-up toys and watch how they move. Wind up each toy as much as you can. Try the toys on different surfaces. Measure how far each one travels.

Which goes the farthest? Why do some travel farther than others? How long does it take each toy to cover the same distance? Which is the fastest? Which is the slowest? What affects the speed? How well does each toy work on the different surfaces?

Nearly four hundred years ago, clock makers
began to use wind-up springs as a way to
store energy for their clocks. This
made it possible for clocks to be made
smaller and to be worn as wristwatches.

Look at this spring-driven watch. Its
gears and levers work together to
move the hands at just the
right speed to measure
time accurately.

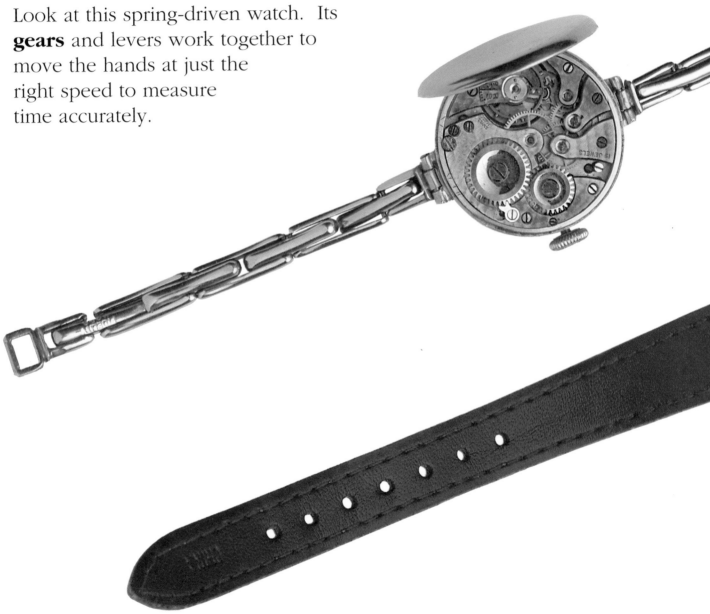

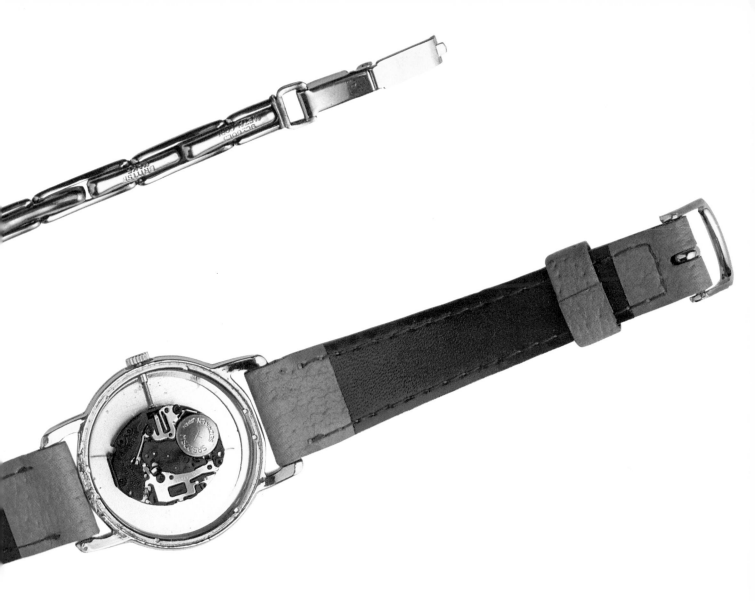

Sixty years ago, the first quartz clock was made. It was very accurate and didn't need winding. Today, many people have quartz watches, like this one, that receive their energy from batteries.

Winding up, winding down

Before clocks had wind-up springs, they worked by a "winding up" of a different kind.

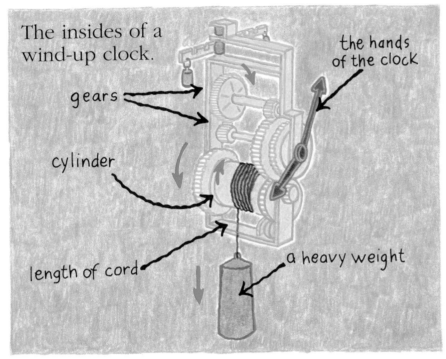

The insides of a wind-up clock.

gears

cylinder

length of cord

the hands of the clock

a heavy weight

The energy that made them work was stored in a raised weight. A length of cord was wound around and around a **cylinder** and attached to a heavy weight. The weight hung freely so that it could fall. Its fall was controlled by gears, making the weight fall in jerks. Each jerk made a ticking sound. The falling weight moved all the clockwork machinery and the clock hands. When the weight reached the end of the cord, someone had to wind it up again to the top.

Place some objects on the edge of a table and push them off onto the floor. (Choose things that won't break!) **Gravity** pulls the objects to the floor. The designers of wind-up clocks knew that the weight at the end of the cord would move downward and that once it reached the ground, the clock would stop. In this type of wind-up clock, energy is added to the weight as it is raised to a high position. The stored energy becomes kinetic energy as the weight falls and turns the cylinder.

Using gravity

You can use gravity to design another kind of spinner. Thread some string through the center of a ball. If you'd like, attach some tassels or fringes to it. Tie the string to a hook overhead so that the ball hangs down.

Twist the string around and around. Where is the energy stored? Then let go, and watch what happens. How long does the ball spin? What happens to the tassels? What kind of energy does the ball have when it is spinning? Try hanging the ball from different lengths of string, or try different sizes and weights of balls. What happens?

Gravity affects the way things move. Try operating this toy from the side. In this position, gravity does not help the acrobat swing through the poles.

A yo-yo is another type of wind-up toy that needs gravity to work. The yo-yo unwinds and begins to spin as you thrust it outward and downward. When it reaches the end of the string, it is spinning fast and begins to wind up the string again. As you move your hand up and down, you give the yo-yo more energy to keep it going.

Try one more toy from the toy box. What energy changes occur when you bounce a rubber ball?

Making a merry-go-round

Now you know something about energy. You know energy is needed to make things work. You know energy can be stored in things like springs and rubber bands. You know that energy can be stored and then changed to kinetic energy to set things in motion.

You know how gravity plays a part in making things move. Its downward pull makes objects fall. You also know about stretching and releasing, tightening and loosening, squeezing and letting go, and winding and unwinding.

Now you can use some of these ideas to help you make a merry-go-round. The plans on pages 30 and 31 will help you.

For a free color catalog describing Gareth Stevens' list of high-quality books, call 1-800-542-2595 (USA) or 1-800-461-9120 (Canada). Gareth Stevens' Fax: 414-225-0377.

The publisher would like to thank Richard E. Haney, Professor Emeritus of Curriculum and Instruction (Science Education) at the University of Wisconsin-Milwaukee for his assistance with the accuracy of the text.

The publisher would like to thank the cover model, Nikki, for her participation.

Library of Congress Cataloging-in-Publication Data

Ollerenshaw, Chris.
    Wind-ups / Chris Ollerenshaw and Pat Triggs. -- North American ed.
      p. cm. -- (Toy box science)
    Includes index.
    ISBN 0-8368-1122-4
    1. Force and energy--Miscellanea--Juvenile literature. [1. Force
and energy.] I. Triggs, Pat. II. Title. III. Series:
Ollerenshaw, Chris. Toy box science.
QC73.4.O45 1994
531'.6--dc20   94-4885

North American edition first published in 1994 by
Gareth Stevens Publishing
1555 North RiverCenter Drive, Suite 201
Milwaukee, Wisconsin 53212 USA

First published in 1991 by A & C Black (Publishers) Ltd., London. Original text © 1991 by Chris Ollerenshaw and Pat Triggs. Additional end matter © 1994 by Gareth Stevens, Inc. All photographs © Peter J. Millard, except p. 7 and p. 14 Mary Evans Picture Library. Model and blueprint by David Ollerenshaw. Illustrations by Dennis Tinkler. Design by Michael Leaman. Cover photograph © 1994 by Jon Allyn, Creative Photographer.

Series editor: Barbara J. Behm
Cover design: Karen Knutson

Printed in the United States of America

1 2 3 4 5 6 7 8 9 99 98 97 96 95 94

At this time, Gareth Stevens, Inc., does not use 100 percent recycled paper, although the paper used in our books does contain about 30 percent recycled fiber. This decision was made after a careful study of current recycling procedures revealed their dubious environmental benefits. We will continue to explore recycling options.

Merry-go-round

Build this working model using a wind-up motor of your own design. You will need a paper plate measuring 7 inches (18 centimeters) across for the base and a brightly colored paper cup for the center support. The revolving top of the model is carried on a Popsicle stick. Photocopy pages 30-31, and then cut out the plans from the photocopy.

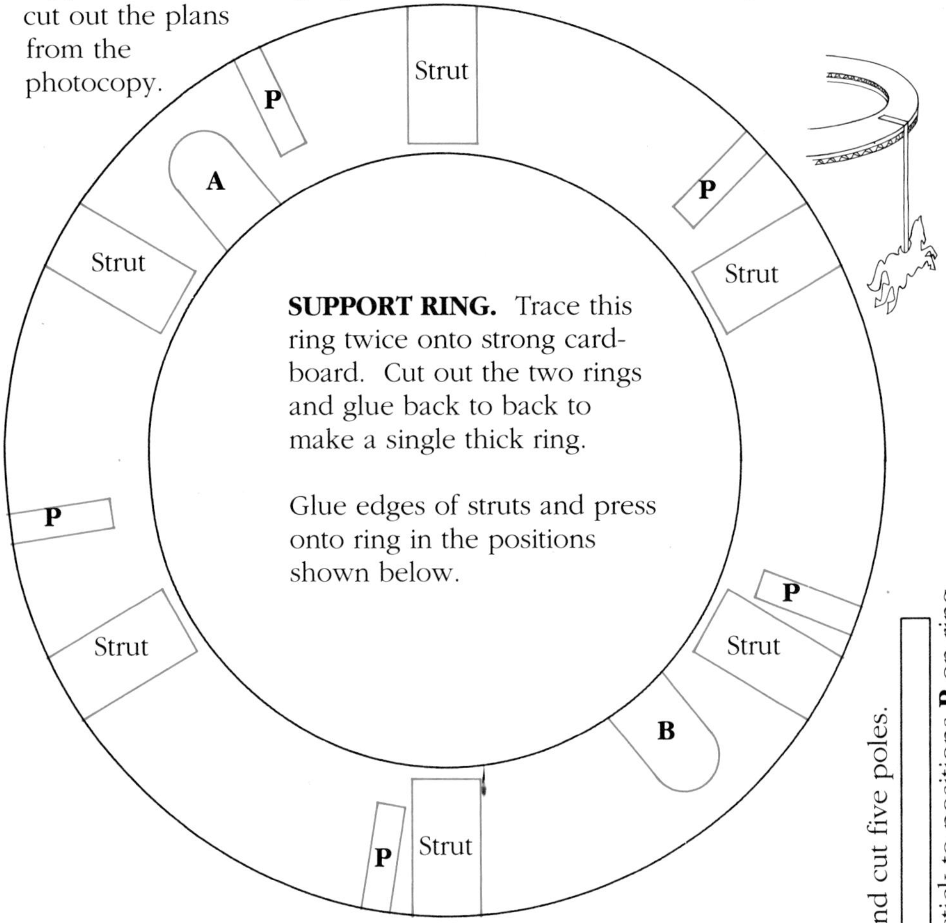

Strut

P

A

Strut

P

Strut

SUPPORT RING. Trace this ring twice onto strong cardboard. Cut out the two rings and glue back to back to make a single thick ring.

Glue edges of struts and press onto ring in the positions shown below.

P

Strut

P

Strut

B

P

Strut

STRUT. Trace six times onto thin cardboard. Cut out, fold, and glue to ring.

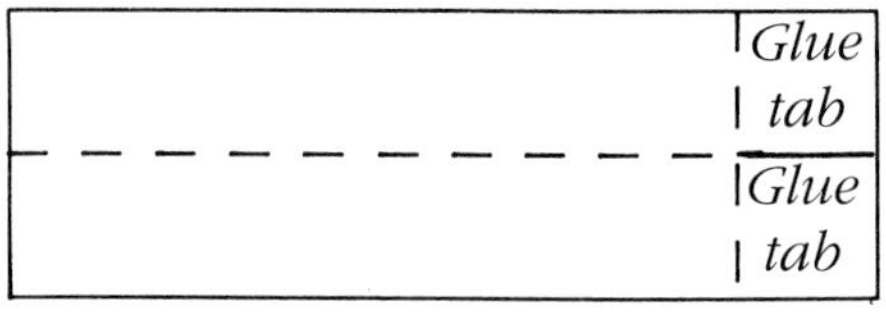

		Glue
		tab
		Glue
		tab

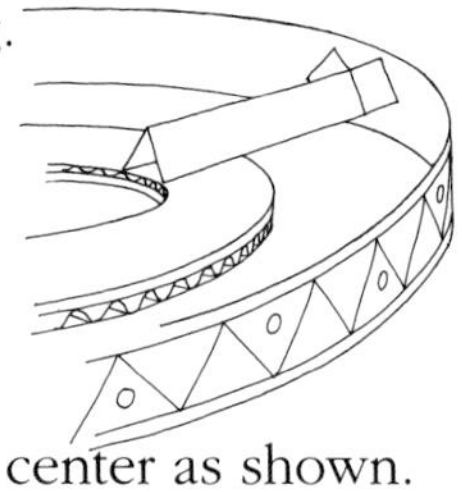

POPSICLE STICK

A   B

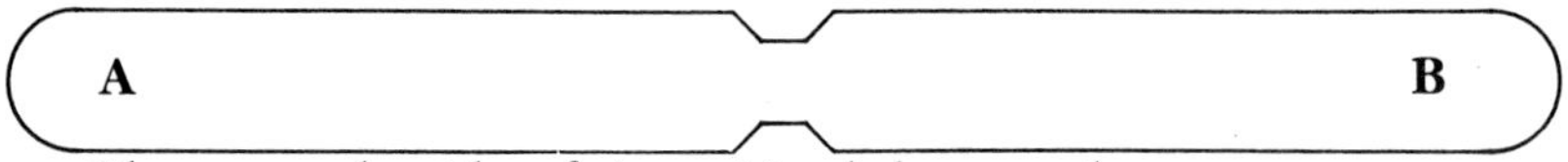

Glue to underside of ring. Match letter to letter.

Shape center as shown.

Bend top of poles over and stick to positions **P** on ring.

TOP BOARD. Trace and repeat the pattern for 22 in. (57 cm). Color. Glue to form circle. Stick to ends of struts.

BOTTOM BOARD. Trace and repeat the pattern for 22 in. (57 cm). Color. Glue to form circle. Then glue around rim of plate.

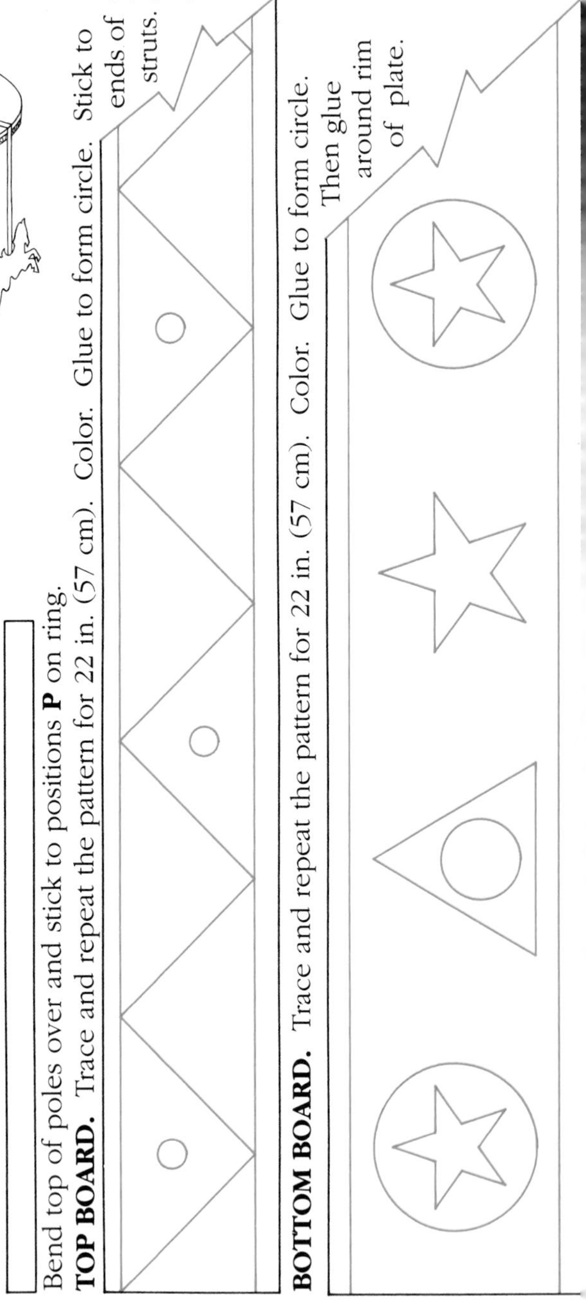

30

TRACE these shapes onto cardboard or paper as directed.
CUT along all solid black lines.

FOLD along all dotted black lines.

GREEN lines show where to glue.
ORANGE lines give ideas for decoration.

ROOFING. Trace and cut out of thick paper. Color before gluing. Do not glue roof to model. Drop into place.

HORSE. Trace and cut five horses out of thick white paper. Leave white. Glue to poles.

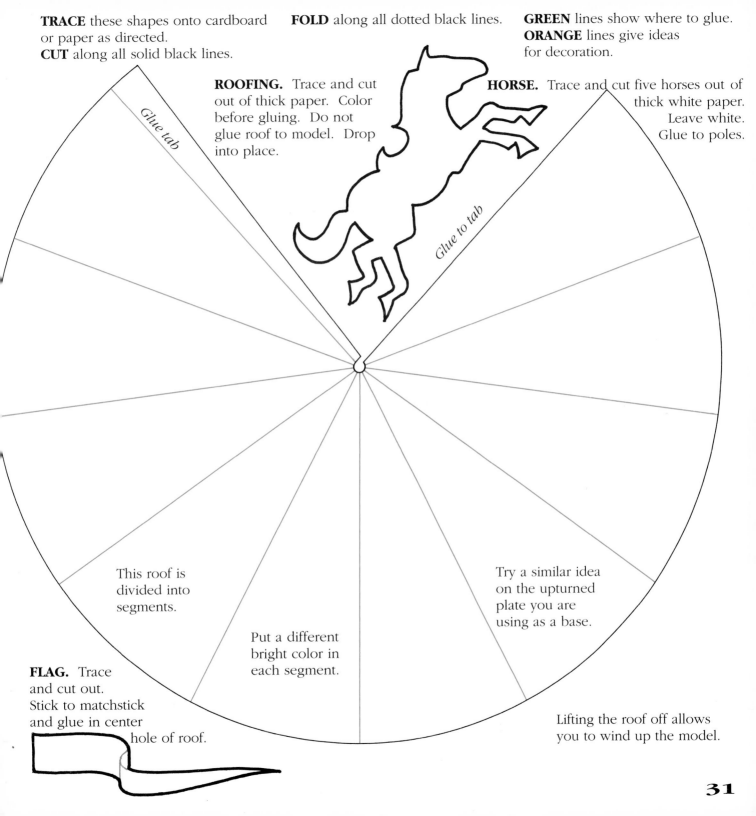

Glue tab

Glue to tab

This roof is divided into segments.

Try a similar idea on the upturned plate you are using as a base.

Put a different bright color in each segment.

FLAG. Trace and cut out. Stick to matchstick and glue in center hole of roof.

Lifting the roof off allows you to wind up the model.

31

Glossary

artificial: not found in nature; made by humans
cylinder: an object shaped like a tube or pipe
energy: usable power for work and play
gears: wheels that fit together to create movement
gravity: the natural force that causes objects to move toward the center of the Earth
kinetic: related to the motion of objects
wind-up: a toy that has a spring wound by hand to make it work

Books and Videos

Energy. Alan Ward (Chelsea Juniors)
Machines and How They Work. Harvey Weiss (Crowell Jr.)
Motion. Joel Leguinn (Creative Education Press)
Simple Machines. Anne Horvatic (E.P. Dutton)

My First Science Video. (Sony video)

Index